# HONG KONG WITHOUT US

T0334465

Georgia Review Books   EDITED BY GERALD MAA

# HONG KONG WITHOUT US

*A People's Poetry*

**EDITED BY THE BAUHINIA PROJECT**

The University of Georgia Press · Athens

© 2021 by the University of Georgia Press

Athens, Georgia 30602

www.ugapress.org

All rights reserved

Designed by Erin Kirk

Set in Warnock Pro

Printed and bound by Sheridan Books

The paper in this book meets the guidelines for
permanence and durability of the Committee on
Production Guidelines for Book Longevity of the
Council on Library Resources.

Photographs by Ping.

Most University of Georgia Press titles are
available from popular e-book vendors.

Printed in the United States of America

25   24   23   22   21   P   5   4   3   2   1

Library of Congress Control Number: 2021931527

ISBN: 9780820360041 (pbk.: alk. paper)

ISBN: 9780820360058 (ebook)

you can't take the streets without first
awakening to your own death—

and most of you: children

# CONTENTS

# FOREWORD

*January 2020*

Before they took Hong Kong in the nineteenth century, the British described it as a "barren rock with hardly a house upon it." Now it is a place of tremendous height and stone, fitting for Sisyphus's fruitless toil. The colonial history says it all, for Hong Kong was colonized twice: first in 1842 as a possession bartered away by the British, and then in 1997 as a possession bartered back by the People's Republic of China (PRC). The latter transaction was not a reunion between Hong Kong and its mother country. By that time, the Chinese Kingdom had been replaced by a new nation-state following two revolutions and a radical overhaul of the old language. Hong Kong was thus a *new* possession, with a distinct language and culture but sharing a distant genealogy. During both transfers of sovereignty, Hong Kong was absent from the bargaining table. Worse, the 1997 transfer came with a promise of fifty years' autonomy before assimilation into the PRC's totalitarian regime. It is hard to imagine a political token more absurd.

Albert Camus gave us an icon of the absurd in his image of Sisyphus: the king stripped of all standing, reduced to a labor without end, left to exalt nothing but the very labor of that laboring. Although Hong Kong still has hardly a house, it has become one of the most densely populated places on earth with its towers and four-walled boxes rising up the slopes. As space dwindles and prices skyrocket, families of four or more cram into two-hundred-square-foot apartments, sharing a showerhead flushing over a toilet in a closet. And, arcing above traffic so cars can go unimpeded, the pedestrian footbridges across Hong Kong have lent it the moniker "city without ground." People live on the highest floors in the smallest rooms and work some of the longest, cheapest hours for an empty, unaffordable future. Add to that a clock ticking toward 2047, and the result is something more circuitously desperate than bare life.

But James Joyce gave us a little more: his image of Sisyphus was one of pure emotion, of rhythmic strain and song as he heaves the boulder to the peak, that distorted breath at the brink between triumph and futility—the origin of the lyric. This book compiles one such lyric. In June of 2019, Hongkongers began taking the streets when their chief executive proposed an extradition bill that would have allowed almost anyone present in Hong Kong to be sent across the border and subjected to the PRC's dubious criminal system. The bill signaled an irreparable early end to the illusion of fifty years' autonomy. In response, millions have come out in demonstration, to be met with mass arrest and a sweeping campaign of misinformation by the PRC that caused even Facebook and Twitter to intervene. Eyes have been shot out by rubber bullets fired by police; hospitals have become danger zones of brutality and abuse; teenagers have been left permanently paralyzed. Those detained at the San Uk Ling Holding Centre reported train rapes in total darkness. Many of those arrested but not charged, whose bodies eventually floated naked into the harbor, were young women. By the close of the year, over seven thousand protesters had been arrested. The vast majority were youths; the youngest was eleven. A dozen protesters have committed suicide. Hundreds have disappeared or been disappeared. And the resistance continues, shapeshifting with each turn.

This book is a glimpse into the movement's lives and voices. The poems here were either submitted as testimonies to the Bauhinia Project through an encrypted email address or collected as "found poems" from testimonies and protest materials on the streets, on social media, and on the news. Each is from an anonymous source and originally written in Chinese. Each was distilled into a few lines of English and hand-made into a postcard to be given as a gift of intimacy to strangers on the other side of the planet. They are a people's poetry: nameless, lowbrow, temporally bound, squeezed out from moments of gravity and strife. They are meant to reach out across the silence of oceans, through differences in language and culture.

A Hongkonger abroad founded the Bauhinia Project as the crisis escalated and it became clear that international media were failing to see Hong Kong on its own terms. The people's demands were simple: withdrawal of the bill, universal suffrage, an independent commission to investigate police misconduct, exoneration for the arrested, and retraction of the "riot" narrative. The extradition bill was finally withdrawn late last year. The establishment was swept out in neighborhood council elections. And a subaltern "yellow economy" has been in the making as the people fend for themselves in a spreading pandemic.

Yet the protests persist with a harder edge. It remains necessary to understand the movement not for its politics, but for its humanity. More than political change, people are demanding a dignified life. They will not drag the stone up the slope—as their parents have long done—just to see it roll back down. They demand a future beyond the fifty-year absurd, and demand to tell their story on their own terms.

The movement is led by children but is "leaderless" in two important ways. First, because all have stepped up equally to take the lead. Second, because by covering their faces they have become fractals of the whole, indistinguishable targets for violence. What was mistaken for the apathy of the young now finds its full expression in a tipping point, in an awakened generation of hopeless children who cannot go on but must go on. That is what makes the movement monumental. Hong Kong is just the whetstone in a greater global crisis; the children who cannot go on are waking up everywhere.

We are suspicious when the arts consume social action, archiving or capitalizing that action while it remains ongoing and urgent. For the Bauhinia Project, art is an ordinary insight: it finds in the profane that which is sacred; it underscores the elemental. Protest and politics are the penultimate profane, which may explain why they are so easily exploited for everyday sensationalism. But we do not believe that Hong Kong is merely a flash in the news, or another notch on the gun of Western democratization. We believe it is no coincidence that, when Hongkongers rose against the beginning of a police state in 2014, people in Ferguson and Bangkok were also rising against the loaded arms of their respective states. We believe that families in Kashmir and Palestine are being silenced by one force that is masked by different faces and insignia. We believe that when the elders in Hawai'i taught us to hold our hands up in a triangle and said, "You are all Mauna Kea," we were learning about much more than the politics of a science project. We believe the seas are rising too fast and bring with them a generation that will no longer roll stones; we believe Greta Thunberg said it best when she asked: Why go to school at all, when world leaders ignore the conclusions of our systems of knowledge? All this is one lyric cry from different mountain peaks. Real solidarity demands that we see each other clearly—now, while we are here, before we fall again.

So, this book is a mirror. It is the promise of a young people coming into being, a promise for what that can mean to a tired world. We are reminded of Aeneas washing ashore in Carthage after fleeing the Trojan War, a devastation of years. In the temple there he is astonished to see depictions of his own friends' deaths in battle. "Sunt lacrimae rerum," he says, and tells his crew to let down their fears: they have arrived safely among a people of mercy, for whom the mortality of things cuts to the heart. They have at last found rest on their long way to founding home. They can forge new strength with the Carthaginians, who too were once refugees, because their stories were told before their coming.

## NOTE ON AUTHORSHIP AND PROCESS

This is an authorless work; and in the end Carthage was destroyed.

The poems in this book are all anonymous and were drawn from multiple sources, many of which have now gone underground. The essays in the volume and the bilingual poems beginning each part were written by the anonymous poets behind the Bauhinia Project. The other poems are denoted as follows:

» These were submitted directly to the Bauhinia Project, previously Tree Hollow Pacific.

~ These were found scrawled or printed on Hong Kong's walls in 2019.

" These were found on digital journalism platforms, including *Apple Daily*, *Stand News*, and RTHK.

= These were found on social media platforms, including Facebook, LIGHK, and temporary Telegram groups.

Part 5 is composed of last wills and testaments, along with dreams for a post-reclamation Hong Kong; the dreams were first crowd-sourced and curated in Cantonese by a social media group that was later renamed and then disbanded because of the National Security Law.

. . . . . . . .

Hong Kong's unique "written Chinese" is a Traditional Chinese text read with a Cantonese inflection. A Taiwanese reader could interpret it visually but not verbally, and a PRC reader of Simplified Chinese would have trouble reading and hearing it. This written, non-colloquial form has survived the city's displacement between colonial languages, finding a poetic home in the lyrics of Cantopop.

Some of the poems were translated directly from this written Chinese. For example, the poem on page 75 is a virtually unedited translation of this email submission:

冰般的少年躺臥
靜止的身體
長出似鱗的海草
從維多利亞港漂去

Teenaged boy like ice
quieted body lying in state
growing scales of seaweed
flowing out from Victoria Harbour

Other poems are translated from another unique language in Hong
Kong, its "written Cantonese." The sources of these poems were
often vernacular, emoji-laden prose testimonies from social media
that were intended for allies and strangers within Hong Kong—
insiders who already share a common emotional understanding.
Our intention was never to make an ethnography of this insiders'
language, nor even to make a literary work of it. Instead, we hoped to
make the emotional understanding available to allies and strangers
outside of Hong Kong, to facilitate a more primordial connection
between the protesters and the rest of the world. For example, the
poem on page 28 originally appeared as this text on an anonymous
Facebook protest account:

想分享一則罷工好人好事，今日遇到一位堅「Be Water」店長：
我剛剛叫左「唐字頭」某盅頭飯外賣，由該分店店長親自送
來，同事輕輕呼籲左句：8月5記得罷工！佢話身為店長，店都
唔開有少少難做，唯有比晒全店同事罷晒工，自己一個人踩全
日😭 仲話：都要開店比D學生食下飯😭大家都係服務業，大家
都係同路人，一切盡在不言中

For illustration only, we provide below a densely literal rendering
to approximate the written vernacular. We have imposed a gender,
although the Cantonese 佢 (unlike the written Chinese 他 or 她) is
gender-nonspecific; we have also left a "typo" intact:

wanna share a good-guy-deed about the strike, ran into a solid
"Be Water" restaurant manager today: I'd just ordered a takeout
rice pail from T——, that the manager delivered himself, [my]
coworker gently call-fending [*sic*]: 8/5, remember to strike! he said
that as the manager, shutting down the whole restaurant was a
lil' hard to do, the only way was to let the coworkers all off to all
strike, [while] himself alone putting pedal to the metal all day 😵
said too: still gotta open the restaurant for dese students to eat a
lil' grub 😵 everyone's in the service industry, everyone's an ally, all
this is beyond words

By paring this down as a short lyric, we sought to reach the quality
that "is beyond words":

"It's the general strike today,"
I gently reminded the delivery man.

He said, "It's hard to close
the whole restaurant.
I let everyone else strike,
only I'm working today.

We have to stay open
to feed students on the street."

He was the manager.

Some would call that adaptation rather than translation. We would
respond that this work refuses language as commodity. Each poem is
like—to paraphrase Walter Benjamin—a call from outside the high
forest to produce a corresponding echo from within it. And because
the leaderlessness of the protests made for a kind of guerilla chorus,
producing gargantuan volumes of personal testimonies that vanished
as swiftly as they appeared, we would say the source text was never
an individualistic, identifiable "I." Rather, the source text was the high
forest itself; it was the human condition in Hong Kong.

We would also highlight our own anonymity and participation in the larger project of Hong Kong's self-determination. We did all this from a sense of urgency alongside the protests, to which the collection that eventually became this manuscript was an afterthought. We culled through thousands of testimonies, whether in screengrabs or in person in Hong Kong, simply to contribute to an evolving transnational dialogue. The resulting poems were distributed as postcards, shared across peoples, and are now still used by speakers to frame panel discussions and events, for a deeper, emotional understanding of Hong Kong. At the same time, our aim was also to translate the people's hearts back to themselves, to show them what their language could be, to show them that they owned it all along. These are not, therefore, poems extracted from a sensational moment for the sake of literature; nor are they poems "about" activism. They are a service for the people, no more and no less.

∙ ∙ ∙ ∙ ∙ ∙ ∙

We thank the *Georgia Review* for publishing an earlier version of the foreword to this volume and several poems in its winter 2019 issue as "Lyric Up the Hills: Postcard Poems from Hong Kong."

The photographs are by someone who wishes to be credited simply as "Ping," who documented the front lines of the protests throughout 2019. We featured those photographs in a medium-pure poetry gallery exhibit, *Hong Kong! Hong Kong!*, which ran from November 22 to December 28, 2019, in Old Oakland. Selected here are a different set of Ping's photographs, of a Hong Kong without protest—a Hong Kong *for whom the protests.*

We return all credit to the journalists and netizens who first interviewed or shared many of the voices distilled here. Most of all we honor the speakers themselves, who were anonymous from the start, whose poems in this book have always been a public good.

| | |
|---|---|
| 天亡 | postmortem sky |
| 血咒　大地起 | blood spell　rising from earth |
| 牢牢大海 | locked-down sea |
| 連根拔起 | yanked by the roots |
| 日蝕盡處 | eye of the eclipse |
| 腳踏行雷 | riding in on thunder |
| 十方湧至 | from the ten directions |
| 吐絲護山 | fold mountains in a gossamer |
| 風眼守 | cyclone-eye guarding |
| 冰凝玉金香 | frozen fresh-gold-jade |
| 曇花不忍 | udumbara flower can't bear it |
| 吐一線曙光 | spits a strand of light |
| 打動 | setting in motion |
| 人間一片胸膛 | an upright mortal coil |
| 千念輪迴 | a thousand thoughts reincarnate |
| 朝天 | heavenward |
| 伸出雙手 | both hands extend |
| \| 不惑 \| | \| sureness \| |
| 萬靈擊掌 | clap of manifold spirits |
| 十指長枝頭 | ten fingers unfurling twigs |
| 嫩芽生 | tender leaves grow |
| 從此 | from here on |
| 不認天地 | disown heaven and earth |

# HONG KONG WITHOUT US

# I

起 · rise

| | |
|---|---|
| 鳥絕 | bird purge |
| 萬靈凝息 | ten thousand souls bating breath |
| 巨鳴 | cosmic bang |
| 三界太月撕裂 | three realms primeval moon shredded |
| 地破天開 | groundburst opening sky |
| 淨水 | chaste water |
| 十方世界湧至 | floods from ten directions |
| 映太初 | reflects the principium |
| 大地 | earth |
| 一片銀河流過 | piece of milky way drifting by |

Both arms scarred
from rubber bullets
now I wear full gear.
It's hard to see clearly
through goggles and lab glasses
but what my future's like
I can't see anyway.

*Anonymous girl* "
*Age fourteen*

Would you accept money
to let them shoot your eye out?

I have no fear.
Better to shoot at me than at girls.
A girl's face is very important.
Better I'm in trouble than someone else.

My hopes and dreams . . .
To grow up sooner!
To be able to drink!
To have a girlfriend!

4

*Anonymous* "
*Age fifteen*

We are not here for fun.
We are the people of Wong Tai Sin
who don't want our home
to be a battlefield.

Rioters? Nine out of ten
are in flip-flops

not even an umbrella.

5

*Anonymous* "
*Age forty*
*Wong Tai Sin*

I fear pain,
I fear death,
I fear I won't see my wife again,
I fear I won't see my kids again,
but I most fear that my kids
cannot see a future.

I am a father.

*Anonymous* =

My mom said if I went out,
she wouldn't let me
back in tonight.

They were still scolding me
when I left. I'm afraid
of cops beating me up

but you can't stop
just because of fear.

Democracy for the people!

*Anonymous* **
*Age ten*
*Shatin*

I watched the teen in full gear
kneeling outside the station
with a cardboard sign asking for
forgiveness. Some patted his back,
left him food and drink. A housewife
with a Mandarin accent told him to get up,

it's the government's fault, not yours.
I came out from my corner
to give him a hug.

I wouldn't have known
that he was shaking,
sobbing behind his mask.

*Anonymous* =

Two million protesters
and still the state
won't give a damn.
They join the gangs,
bleed our city's kids.

This is no longer my Hong Kong!

If I were to die now
my eyes would never close.

*Anonymous* »
*Age seventy-four*
*Tai Hang Road*

Seventeen now,
just twenty-seven when I'm out of jail,
maybe by then Hong Kong's illness
will be gone
I'm sorry Hongkongers,
I'm just a high schooler,
the cops are stronger than me,
I couldn't protect anyone
but I could smother canisters
of tear gas for you

*Anonymous girl* =
*Age seventeen, with* PTSD

From the teargassed street
into a restaurant
I asked if I could charge my phone.
He asked if I wanted to eat.
I had no money left.

*Anonymous* =

Going to the protests on my own?
Well, we come to this world alone
and leave alone. We are always alone.
Why be afraid?

This summer taught me
nothing's absolute.

I just want to be someone
who will change society
when I grow up.

*Anonymous* "
*Age fourteen*

Can you escort me home?
I have things in my backpack
I need to hide from the cops.
Wait here, I want a chocolate shake.
Some rice noodles too.

No, not yet. I've only eaten
tear gas today. I fainted last time
when a canister hit my chest.

Why be afraid?
It's just a few years behind bars.
Life would be the same anyway.

*Anonymous* "
*Age twenty*
*Shatin*

I'm just a housewife.
Last night I joined a rally,
it was pouring,

when I looked up
an umbrella was shielding me,
raised by a teen.

*Anonymous* =

As a civil servant, I serve
my people. But look—

Two million marched—ignored.
Our teens bled in the front—condemned.
Cops joined hands with gangs—condoned.
And you—still dodging our demands.
I warn you: the city's mailmen will join Monday's strike.

We apologize to Hongkongers
for the inconvenience.

*Anonymous* =

I left twenty bucks to a homeless man
bore his cardboard shield
and hurled a small rock.
The police raised their rifles
and aimed at my head.

*Anonymous* "

It's not politics anymore
just conscience.
Yes the government
can do anything now,
imprison, torture, sue,
but they can't go back
to how things were.

Without conscience
a lot of people could be harmed
by a former drug dealer like me
even single-handedly

not to say by a government.

*Anonymous* =

投 · cast

| | |
|---|---|
| 黑山火起 | black hills fires rise |
| 微草佇立 | a slight grass stands |
| 延天地萬里 | fanning out over land and sky |
| 空天空 | empty empyrean |
| 煙火 | fumes |
| 若即若離 | neither coming nor leaving |
| 雲崩 | avalanche clouds |
| 棄天 | abandoning heaven |
| 投大地夢 | cast into earth's dream |
| 偏木緩開 | endwood languishes open |
| 煙消火逝前 | ere slaking fume and flame |
| 拾人間灰燼 | culling mortal coil |

He looked like any elementary schooler
munching a bun before the march.

I asked him why his gas mask
had no filters.

He said he put them in
only when necessary.
They were too expensive.

He put on his helmet,
which couldn't fit however we adjusted it.
His head was too small.

He knocked on it a few times,
grimaced—

"Guess it's enough."

*Anonymous* “

They think we're high school dropouts.
I was making 42k a year

when I witnessed protesters attacked.
I quit my job out of guilt.

Our squad targets cops
and gangsters.

What connects us?
Broken homes and no families

so we'll die to protect our home,
Hong Kong.

*Anonymous* "
*Age twenty-one*
*"Dragon Slayers" squad*

I fight in the front, so what?
I've seen girls of my age too.
I'll never forget my first time:
when I stepped out from the subway
people squirmed on the ground
their legs covered in blood.
I was born in Hunan
so here they call me locust.
But in this fight, I have been here.

*Anonymous* **"**
*Age fourteen*

Taking tear gas is painful,
my pee came out red.
Rubber bullets are painful too,
my bruise took a week to fade.

Dad doesn't know where I went
but Mom supports me.
She even made fun of where I was shot—
my butt!

*Anonymous* "
*Age fifteen*

Coming home from a day of tear gas
my mom grabbed my hair, slapped me,
asked if I'm a pro-independence asshole.

I've spent eighteen years with my parents,
who've never supported anything I do

but these strangers in the street
give me a dignity I've never had.

This fancy gas mask was a gift
from a sister first-aider.

In the bank now I have
less than two bucks.

I won't give in.

*Anonymous* "
*Age eighteen*
*Tin Shui Wai*

I was born here, but as a South Asian
I never thought I could call myself
a Hongkonger, till the day I was arrested
with another boy. He asked if my parents
were coming. I shook my head.
"Don't worry, my dad is coming,
he'll bail you out too!"

*Anonymous* "
*Age fifteen*

It's exactly because I'm a mother,
it's for the next generation.

Even if I'm arrested,
I'm not a rioter, I'm a fighter.

I always tell my daughters:
if something's right, do it now.

*Anonymous* "

"It's the general strike today,"
I gently reminded the delivery man.

He said, "It's hard to close
the whole restaurant.
I let everyone else strike,
only I'm working today.

We have to stay open
to feed students on the street."

He was the manager.

*Anonymous* =

The restaurant suddenly took in
a crowd dressed all in black.
Free dishes came endlessly out.

The police broke in
but only found teens
and neighbors, their outfits
changed, eating together.

*Anonymous* =

Hong Kong's an old friend
I've never met. I'm so lame I couldn't
even protect the three lychee trees
my grandpa planted. But I want to stand
together with you.
Just like the young man said
biking that picturesque day
in Beijing, 1989.
This is my albatross.
The day I finally meet Hong Kong
I'll tell her all about these years
and then leave again without lifting
one grain of dust.

*Anonymous* =
*Age twenty-seven*
*Guangxi, China*

You see the handwriting? A perfect imitation. Every time they tear down the Lennon Wall, I dig the words out from the trash, bring them home, and copy them by hand. I started at 3 a.m. last night, then took the first morning train to put them back up.

But I can't reproduce the kids' drawings.

Don't worry, I'm not a bad guy.
I'm just a security guard.
I want to protect our people's dreams.
Even if they're just on paper.

*Anonymous* =

—Big sis, look what I drew.
—Big sis can't tell what it is.
—It's a protester beaten to death by police.
—Then what's the black thing?
—It's a shield.
—Why would he die if he had a shield?
—Because it's made of paper.

*Anonymous* =
*Age five*
*Airport*

Every time, I bring my last will
and testament. I was suicidal until
this protest. Now I'm optimistic.
At one protest I was lectured for four hours
by an old man. "Dying is nothing
but one should die meaningfully."

My shield is made of seven compressed
boogie boards. I was still captured
by riot police as I pushed away two teens
standing in a daze. Later the cops said
I'm not a bad kid.

Hong Kong is our home.
If we don't fight for her, who will?

Sigh.

I don't want to go back to school.

*Anonymous* **"**
*Age fifteen*

His backpack has spray paint,
a helmet, gloves, a tennis racquet.
"For fighting back tear gas."

"Actually," he blurts,
"I was arrested already."

He just wants to skateboard after school.
His backpack also has his last will
and testament, in which he imagines
a Hong Kong without him.

*Anonymous* "
*Age fourteen*

They say I'm too young to understand,
they say I'm brainwashed.

I say what motivated me to go out
was all your lies, adults.

I only believe what I see.
I was at the 8/11 mass arrest.

*Anonymous* =
*Age thirteen*

He was beaten in a pool of blood
when he ran back to save other protesters.
They were undercover cops.

*Anonymous* =

Three hundred squatting outside the wet market
wielding racquets, umbrellas, traffic cones,
and stainless-steel steamed-fish plates,
waiting to smother another round of teargas.
Behind them a thousand evacuating.

One is injured, sent to the back for care.
Another moves forward, takes his place.

*Anonymous* =

My friends said
let's join the protests in Hong Kong.
I declined carefully.
They were going to "support" as tourists
while Hong Kong people
actually put their lives on the line.
I want to stand with these people
not as a tourist
but as a sister.

*Anonymous* »
*Age twenty*
*Berkeley, California*

Even the heavens have a sunset to lead the way,
even a perfect storm can't hold back the rain

*Anonymous ~*
*Tai Po Lennon Wall*

# 執 · hold

| | |
|---|---|
| 千年影 | thousand-year shadow |
| 求牆之巔 | hounding the tip of the wall |
| 夢晃 | pendulous dream |
| 送千年光 | sends thousand-year light |
| 無極之力 | infinity knot |
| 毀千年寒夢 | ruins the thousand-year brumal dream |
| 霧纏山石 | fog fettering crag |
| 執天地永恆 | holding fast to everlasting sky and land |
| 一念隨 | a single thought follows |
| 水起 | waters rise |
| 天滅人間 | heaven smothers mortal coil |

I live in subsidized housing
on the thirtieth floor.
Every night here it's the same dude
chanting, "Reclaim Hong Kong,
Revolution of Our Time."

Tonight, I couldn't wait for him
any longer. I shouted out my window,
"Hongkongers, Courage!"

The echo came back
from neighbors in my tenement
and from the luxury towers
across the way.

43

*Anonymous* **=**

In our tenement, we screen
videos of the protests.
Everyone comes with soda
in flip-flops.

In a leaderless movement
if you just make the first step

you'll see there's something
you can do, for everyone.

*Anonymous* =

I've done pro bono work for a decade
and have never seen arrestees
like these teens. Not "help me,"

but: "I'm fine. Help the younger ones."
"Help him first. He doesn't have an attorney."

*Anonymous* "

When I saw riot police waiting
on the platform I wondered if I should skip
the station. I didn't want to see
another tragedy. As the passengers
waited to get out, I finally opened
the train doors, announcing:
*Passengers, please pay special attention.*
*I repeat, passengers, please pay special*
*attention when alighting from the train.*

A woman passed the conductor's car
holding a sheet that read, "Gratitude."

*Anonymous* =
*Lai King Station*

While I'm here no kid will go hungry.
As long as I'm needed I'll cook.
I can't fight, I just make food.
I'm a chef: feeding people
is my life's purpose—

and this bandanna of the U.S. flag?
It's my dream of freedom.

*Anonymous* "
*Chinese University of Hong Kong & Hong Kong Polytechnic University*
*during both police sieges*

He was middle-aged,
leaning on a handrail,
watching the riot police
listlessly from a few blocks
away. He lived upstairs;
his son was in the front line.

*Anonymous =*
*Sai Ying Pun*

A mother desperately screamed
her son's name into the crowd.

"Your son is not here!"
A police officer

pepper-sprayed her in the face.

*Anonymous* "

How can you not be angry?
Even my students got beaten up!
To pay me now would be an insult.

Our people have only themselves.

All I know is an everyman's martial art.
It's my duty to advance it for all.

*Anonymous "*
*Wing Chun sifu*

Our forebears, modest, decent, were genteel
villagers. We are the proud indigenous
New Territorians. Even the Brits respected us.

Today's thugs are not ours.
Fellow indigenous people: we stand
together to defend our blood's
moral compass, our dignity.

*Anonymous* =
*New Territories*

I went down for a beer after work.
The kid in line didn't have enough
for the cheapest bun. I asked to pay
for him. He turned me down.
I gave him four hot dogs
and asked if he wanted anything else.
Stubbornly, no. Then,

"Uncle." I turned around.
"Thank you."

He pulled out his phone
and took a selfie with me.

*Anonymous* =

I only have three bucks.
Can you take me to the farthest subway stop?

My leg? I sprained it
when cops stormed the mall.

Eighth grade, after this summer. I told my parents
I was going to play video games with a friend.

Why? Because it's so unjust that everything
we do is wrong, and everything they do is right!

I'm only afraid of being arrested
because I don't want my family to know.

But I didn't do anything wrong.

*Anonymous* "
*Age thirteen*

Two grannies sit in court every day
with Buddhist scriptures.
When the two teen defendants
came out today, they began to pray,
eyes closed, rolling their rosaries.

*Anonymous* =

After my court hearing
a girl was crying, blaming herself
for leaving early that night.

But I am not guilty.
I stood true.
          Sister,
don't blame yourself.

Take up my part in the fight.
And save your tears for the day
we finally pull down our masks
and see each other.

*Anonymous* =

A bus rescue from the police siege on protesters at the airport, stuck in traffic, four hours to gain a few miles, each seat packed with two or three persons:

—This bus was made in China . . .
—Sit on the floor. It won't tip over as easy.
—The cab next to us, its meter's at $400 already.
—I'll call food delivery for everyone. A moped could easily catch up.
—The bus is turning! Everyone, shift your balance a little to the right.
—I told my parents I was at hotpot. Anyone have a hotpot pic?
—Google it. They won't fact-check.
—I have one. Airdropping you now.
—What's the hotpot place called?

*Anonymous* ▪

In a decentralized movement
surrounded by danger
to trust a stranger so much
that you get in his car
and stay in his home
it shows the great extent
of your hopelessness.

I never liked hosting guests
but after the kid who killed himself
when his parents kicked him out
I open my door to everyone.

*Anonymous* =

I couldn't face myself if I stayed home
when those outside are younger than me.

I should've had a summer job by now,
a normal life after graduating,

but because of this protest
I discovered I'm not someone

who retreats when others retreat,
who charges when others charge—

I stand on my own two feet.

*Anonymous* "
*Age eighteen*

After the tear gas
a big guy in full gear
tottered through the crowd
holding, on a sheet of paper
from the garbage,
a baby gecko.

He handed it to me,
said bring it to safety,

and even after I left
looked on in longing.

*Anonymous* =

On the platform
an eleven-year-old, alone,
shy, yellow raincoat, face mask,
goggles. He inched toward me.

He'd lied to come out
and didn't know how to get home
because the subway lines had changed.

When we arrived
I patted his head.

It was the size of my hand.

*Anonymous* =

"Free tickets! Free tickets!"
subway staffer at the gate
evacuating crowd

*Anonymous* =

At the night protest, two teens
sat with their heads in their phones
with the flashlight on

to expose a step in the darkness,
to brighten the way.

*Anonymous* =

## INTERLUDE

A place may be no more than its people. But the people of your past, for so long burned to ash because there was no room to be buried, gave you no thought as they passed through. And of the people today, how do we sort those who've left from those who cannot leave, and those who choose to stay? A place may be no more than land. Today that means a price per square foot; bodies of water daily seen but unnoticed; a soil coated in cement; a sliver of sky each child sees while looking up between towers. A place may be renamed, layered over, erased: New York a replanting of British York, from Roman Eboracum, over lands still fought for by survivors of five older nations, the Haudenosaunee, whose ancestors were made to live elsewhere. If the people leave you to make a home on a different land, then which land is you?

You were a useless rock, the hybrid worst and pearl of East and West, harbor at the farthest edge where Chinese rebels, exiles, and refugees made their home. You were a home to Brits who failed in London, then Europeans who came to your city of corners to cut and unmake their pasts. You took the unwanted and unfit, the illegal immigrants, the lost and homeless, spat out from both ends of the earth, who sought a limbo between shadows. And now some even look to you with longing—a spiritual home. Some even call themselves exiles from a country that doesn't exist yet.

It's the children of all these outcasts who were raised on your breast. It's they who punch holes in the cement, finding your soil, planting roots. It's they who rescue saplings the adults tore down, who care for each drop of polluted rainwater, who bask in sunlight blocked by the high-rises their parents built, who care even for the geckos that are left behind injured. It is they who have no past to escape, who have known only you all their life. Theirs is not a generation of failing in one place to flee to another. They fight. They would rather die than give up their home. And when they do, they are made to float on a layer of trash above the water, to lie on the cement and be still an inch away from your soil. They call themselves Hongkongers. Bring them into yourself. Bring them home.

# IV

滅 · extinguish

| | |
|---|---|
| 幻起象默 | rising mirage silencing form |
| 萬月迴向 | manifold moon offertory |
| 彼岸 | the Other Shore |
| 水形空 | shape of water emptied |
| 霧勢磅礴 | august mist |
| 晴空血日 | clear skies blood sun |
| 天要行刑 | heaven must execute |
| 光明頂 | the brilliant crowns |
| 外天邊之凜 | austere beyond the sky's edge |
| 山巒綿綿 | wrinkle of silk peaks |
| 千眼 | like a thousand eyes |
| 俯瞰千年 | staring down a thousand years |

How many sleepless nights
chasing around a city
of endless high-rises
scrying for one building
from a single photograph
in which we saw a kid standing
on the edge of the roof?

*Anonymous* "

I heard a voice shout,
"Reclaim Hong Kong!"
Then a loud noise.
Then the medical personnel
downstairs with a body bag.

*Anonymous* =

Teenaged boy like ice
quieted body lying in state
growing scales of seaweed
flowing out from Victoria Harbour

*Anonymous* »
*Age forty-six*
*Taikoo*

My teenaged son was brought back
by cops for a midnight house search.
When I opened the door I fumed
to see him handcuffed.
                    Then: "Mom,
can you push my glasses up a little?"
As I drew near
he kissed me on the forehead.

*Anonymous* "

A young man chanted slogans nearby
at ten every night. Honestly, his voice
was hoarse and too loud. It always
woke my kids up. But when I didn't hear
anything, I thought he'd been arrested
or murdered.

He came back at last.

I'd rather you wake us every night
than have these sleepless nights
of worry.

*Anonymous* =

How many of us out there
with this chemical smell
from head to toe, who wait alone
in the back stairwell
until everyone falls asleep
before going home?

*Anonymous* =

My cab's been dented twice
by tear gas canisters.

But one day I saw two
young girls outside 7-Eleven
sharing a cup of instant noodles
on the curb. I left them thirty bucks.

What can I do?
I'm just a cab driver.

*Anonymous* =

My husband said, "Hardship can make a person surrender. I just need a wife who supports me unconditionally." He's a policeman.

I'm not afraid
to be a single mother
as long as my child
lives free, not in fear.

*Anonymous* "

A seventy-year-old grandma
with Alzheimer's, holding my hand
in the human chain, told me she would wear
a suicide bomb and run into the government complex
if that would win this battle for Hong Kong.

She hugged me three times,
didn't let my hand go till the end.

*Anonymous* =

I grew up here. How could the cops behave like this? It could only be because they're afraid. Well, even I went downstairs, but only because my neighbors returned in tears.

*Anonymous* »
*Age seventy*
*Wong Tai Sin*

These six months, Dad,
I've told many lies.

After setting roadblocks
and standing down tear gas

I would pat myself
in cheap vodka, head to toe,
before coming home.

You think I'm an alcoholic
but two beers would get me drunk.

If anything happens
open my Google Drive
and read my will there.
Password: my name, your number.

I really wished that one day
I'd hear you say you supported me,
even just once.

*Anonymous* **=**

Everyone says we fight for the next
generation—but not me. I fight
for my mother. To protect her future
with hope. I don't sacrifice
for bravery, but for my love of her.

After six stitches
to my head, I called
to hear her voice. I hoped
she would pick me up.

She said my blood
would stain her bed—
if I had to, just don't die
inside her home.

*Anonymous* "
*Age seventeen*

He asked me to keep his will
to give to his single mom if anything happened.
She'd kicked him out for protesting.

"If all the youth are killed," he said,
"who then is the next generation?"

*Anonymous* "

—Who's on duty today?
—Me, sir.
—Who wrote this on the blackboard?
—Not sure. I can clean it for you, sir.
—I'll ask again: who wrote this on the blackboard?
—Don't rouse suspicion! Don't cleave the mat! Don't be a rat! Sir!
—Stop applauding, everyone shut up! One last time: who wrote this on the board? It's your duty to keep an eye on it between classes.
—Don't rouse suspicion, don't cleave the mat, don't be a rat. I have nothing else to say, sir.
—Pack your stuff and go to detention.
—Sir, I'm on strike today. I'll go with him.
—Sir, I'm not well today.
—I'll have to miss this class too.

And sing along the way:

*Children of our just path, revolution of our time*
*Entreat democracy, freedom, ten thousand lives undying*
*May there glory to Hong Kong be*

*Anonymous* =

I wouldn't have known that riding
on the Tuen Mun highway would one day
be such joy, even in a police van.
I'm an ordinary college kid,
far from wise, mostly lazy,
and who isn't afraid of
bleeding, beatings, arrest?
But look at all these teens running
for their lives through the smoke
when they should be on a court
playing basketball. It's conscience.
The thoughts keep radiating out
until they find an echo.
So see y'all soon
after these years behind bars.

*Anonymous* "

He's a frontliner: for six months
we haven't seen each other,
haven't had time to talk.
He wouldn't let me come to Hong Kong.
The first day he took the streets,
he awakened to his own death.
If I didn't hear from him,
I'd search for his name
among the lists of arrestees.
Before going out he always wrote, "I love you."
Our chat has no words, just hundreds of days
of I love you, and those double tick-marks in blue.

*Anonymous* =
*Taiwan*

I was teargassed with my two kids today.
In the chaos some teens evacuated us.
They stood in front so we could run.
I couldn't see their faces.

I remember their strong scent—
like gunpowder.

*Anonymous* =
*Kwai Fong*

# V

生 · birth

| | |
|---|---|
| 極夢 | dream of dreams |
| 點小溪 | dotting the little creeks |
| 萬行之初 | dawn of ten thousand deeds |
| 石影盡 | stone's shadow's end |
| 路不能移 | the path can't be moved |
| 人疾風疲 | man afflicted wind wearied |
| 大地 | the earth |
| 一片黃沙肅清 | yellow sand expunged |
| 萬世轉 | ten thousand lives revolve |
| 如空空替 | empty replacing empty |
| 換人間 | swap out this mortal coil |
| 一草之善 | one grassleaf of grace |

"

My beloved city, may glory be to you. My goodbye letter is in my backpack. In the next life . . . if there's a next life, let me take a look at you again.

**I want to plant more trees, make fresher air for Hong Kong!**

**My dream is to have and join our own army. I want to protect Hong Kong!**

What will come is probably a revolution made from piles of dead bodies. I don't know how long I'll stay alive. If, one day, I'm said to have committed suicide by jumping off a building, or I become a floating body in the river, I must have been murdered by the police because I won't commit suicide. I'll fight to my last breath.

**I want to be an engineer and re-build a Hong Kong that truly belongs to Hong Kong people.**

**" "**

I have no regrets, even if my body is smashed and my bones are ground to powder. If anything happens to me and I don't come home again, please don't be sad. Because your daughter, your granddaughter, left the world holding on to what she believed in.

**I only want to own a corner store so I can sit outside and say hi to my neighbors every day.**

**My dream is to see every Hongkonger smile.**

**I want to be a translator who can connect Hong Kong with the rest of the world.**

Dad, I'm sorry for leaving you so soon, and for not doing my job of taking care of you as a son. If I leave before you, please take good care of yourself.

**My dream is to build bike lanes across the city, so our lives won't be trapped by vehicles and the traitorous subway system.**

**"  "**

If I told you I wasn't afraid, I'd be lying. But we can't give up because of that.

**My dream is that when I get home after work, I won't even need to lock the door. We'll trade dinner dishes with our neighbors, sometimes dessert and soup too. We'll leave our doors open, chant some slogans together, and chat.**

When you see this letter, I've probably been arrested, or murdered.

**My dream is to open a school and replace our banking model of education with a real education that lets our kids grow up happily instead of committing suicide.**

**My dream is to open a restaurant that hires only political prisoners.**

In fact, I'm really afraid of death, and that I won't see you again. I'm worried you'll cry for me. Or you'll collapse. But I have to go out.

95

**"    "**

Grandma, remember to take your medicine on time. Dad, don't fall asleep on the couch anymore. I promise that I'll do my best to pay you all back in my next life. I'm very sorry.

**I want to franchise McDonald's so I can give every kid the biggest ice cream and a giant box shoved full of fries. I'd also open the restaurant for people in need to stay there at night.**

**My dream is to be a good civil engineer, building affordable homes for Hong Kong people.**

**My dream is very simple: I want to be a mother. I want to be free from the fear of having kids.**

My last hope, even though you can't understand why I took the streets, is that you will forgive my stubbornness, and make my bravery your pride. Thank you.

**My dream is to open a tailor shop that fixes people's clothing, so we can change our city's deep-seated, morbid consumerism.**

**"  "**

**I want to be a teacher without borders and help other children in the world.**

**After reclaiming Hong Kong, I want to invent the best Hong Kong bun in the world, and make animations for children to watch after their homework time is strictly cut off at 5:15 p.m.**

Every time I step through the door, my parents ask me not to go out. But I can't leave my brothers and sisters alone out there. I can't leave my people out there. I have to stand with them.

I hope one day my family will understand me. I am not taking the streets for myself. I'm fighting for Hong Kong, for our city's children, and for our future.

**My dream is to clean up Hong Kong's water so we can even scuba-dive in our Victoria Harbour!**

**My dream is to be a cat photographer and an artist. Not a real estate agent anymore.**

Who then taught me
to use sticky notes
like fractured bones
to tattoo on the city's walls
where blood flows like
the red lines of a maze.

When silence stabs my eyes
star clusters explode in a vacuum
the night song at ten always wakes me
as someone in this world pains my pain
a hundred, a thousand times.

Exile yourself to the street, dear,
it's our only way home.

*Anonymous* ∼
*Chinese University of Hong Kong*

# AFTERWORD

No reason to lump you here, Roberto Bolaño, seventeen years gone, in a poetry book about Hong Kong. You would not have liked the city's meager paean to Latin America, the one or two taquerias in the sloped alleys of the expat quarters. The ghost-men rave there between bites, adrift in spirits, flirting in English while across the harbor smoke fills the streets and children run for their lives in Cantonese. Meanwhile, in the Chile you left, in the Santiago where neoliberalism laid its first golden egg: a mutilation of eyes, young masses blinded by shots of rubber and tear gas, cries of a people spiraling back to Pinochet. And more, across your Costa Brava, your wife and son's Catalonia, the Mediterranean with your ashes: secession, suppression, police and their weapons. But, everywhere *llibertat* too. In Catalonia they chanted slogans from Hong Kong. In Hong Kong they flew Catalan flags. On a radio in America: "no police brutality" in Spanish, then in Cantonese, behind the interviews back to back.

In America, one lost Hongkonger found you, molding in a warehouse of salvaged goods, two dollars for a yellowed lifetime of words. She traced you from desert to desert, beach to beach, as though ludic worldliness could cleanse the palette of having left your first coast, as though you were still on the chase, as hesitant to say "home" as she would be, reluctant of the word's privilege. Later, she went to a solidarity night for Chile, sat comfortably in the front where she thought no one could see her face. And you were not there. You were not the poet who kicked off the night by reading Pablo de Rokha, nor the artist flying in to report from Santiago. You were not the interpreter sitting beside her struggling to keep up, not the singer tap-dancing on stage. You were not anyone in the audience applauding in a lonely fever, not anyone chanting in Spanish. You were not the old woman who shook her hand and thanked her at the end, so surprised to see an Asian face supporting a people abroad in a language she could not speak. There was no place for you there, dead foreigner poet with no homeland left but language. You could only have been there with her, alive in her as she wondered if James Joyce—who left Ireland forever after being punched unconscious on a street in Dublin over a dumb misunderstanding—would have returned if born into the Troubles? Would you? Would she?

She was just a drunk once, back in Hong Kong, with no one to pick her up from the pier, just a fool writing on the cigarette cartons in her pockets, on napkins greased from takeout on the ferry home after work. Each time she flew back for the protests last year, gathering the streets' unbearable lines, she stayed in an hourly hostel near home. On Father's Day, her father did not know she had returned. She was a precursor to this young generation, whose great fear is not police torture but the cell of home, the parents who will not understand and will beat them for wanting to know beauty, then beat them again for wanting to know justice. For to know one is to know the other.

When Chinese peasants arrived at the station on Angel Island and their desperation trailed into the fitful fume of years, they started carving poems. Their lines are still on the walls, radiating with lead poison in the exposed wood, layered by the putty and paint that the maintenance staff thought could unmake a chink graffiti. But when Chinese peasants arrived in Hong Kong, which was invented for no other reason than to blast open a market between empires, the people started carving vulnerability out of themselves, carved their bodies into numbers. How bereft, living to serve a machine that cannot see you. Becoming smooth and cold, mimicking that machine, adopting its accent, loathing your own people. Even to be assigned readings like *The Woman Warrior* in school, as though your colonizers had mistaken you for immigrants desperate to invent an ancestral home, as though it were not already the factory bleeding across the border. How could poetry ever be homegrown in Hong Kong, when literature is just another costume of colonization, when poems sit rotting in the most secret cells of people's hearts?

It is not the people's fault to lack words, even with journalists. It is not their fault when, short of statistics and the emoji of a face with tears, they can only articulate a life in Hong Kong by jumping out of a window. In subsidized housing, children are told not to linger downstairs too long in case someone jumps from above. Even right now a child is dreaming of an iron umbrella strong enough to deflect bodies, beneath which to go on playing. It's said that the only time a tree knows freedom is when it leaves its parent as a winged seed, flying off to plant roots not far from home. In Hong Kong, some people are free only when they fly from the rooftops. Then the street is cleaned, the road unblocked, and the body becomes a number again on the news. The hamster is replaced. The wheel spins again. A grief that leaves no mark, no trail anywhere. No root even for a word of sorrow.

Yet poetry is absent elsewhere, too. The Boom you hated is alive and well. The fool's paradise of the MFA has made an industry of smokestacks: AWP, international workshops and conferences, awards invented for the sake of advertisement, tenure-track positions of nervous masturbation. You would be unsurprised by the latest social media erotica: poets taking selfies with their books. Somewhere tonight, Bolaño, a poet sucks complimentary boba through a straw at the end of a long day of washing dishes and sees you writing on the floor after a night of collecting garbage, while outside the wars continue numbly, the poles melt, wildfires turn the sky to nuclear haze, and a spreading virus turns the human face into a weapon of terror. New technology postpones death while more people than ever are forced into the streets, hungry beside locked dumpsters stuffed with food. The human herds are shoved into narrow commutes, inventing noise-canceling headphones to create walls of sound. The herd has become so clever that it has only itself left in a world of neo-nihilism, a world crumbling on screen.

This is a time of sirens. The ancients knew when they had plundered too much from nature, and they believed they could reset the balance by sacrificing innocents. Today the innocents commit suicide; they throw themselves headlong into the asphalt of unstoppable progress. They learn of five million animals dying in Australia's five-month fire while listening to the neighbors fuck upstairs and throw condoms out the window. There is a song to hear here, inviting the most heroic to jump ship or be tied down to mast. This is a time for real combat, a time for poets. A time to live. Bolaño, you thought that inside each person is the abyss. But no: look at the children today, at their convulsive dance. They are the tree falling to announce the forest. Inside each person is a forest.

In Hong Kong, there's an old story about a toddler at Exchange Square. While other children played around the fountain, this child squatted between the bronze water buffaloes. A stream of white clouds passed overhead at maniacal speed. The child thought the planet was spinning too fast. That once Hong Kong reached the bottom, she would fall from the earth and into space. She then realized that her stuffed animals, her chicks and bunny, her mother and sister, everyone in Hong Kong would also fall from the earth. She sank into that deep eye of transition, that dark space from which she alone worried for the human race. Sucked into the void, chest pained, eyes pooling, she fumbled to clutch the marble surfaces around her, as though they could be leaves of grass, as though they could speak and hold her. She strained to stop the world from its uncontrollable spinning. She stared at the clouds so ardently that they began to break her mind, break her language.

The story stops there. For at that moment her mother arrived, looking just fine, no idea what was happening to the celestial maps. The mother dragged her away to finish the next errand. And it broke the girl's heart. And the world went on spinning.

Bolaño, that girl was me. That girl was Hong Kong.

# POSTSCRIPT: AFTER THE NATIONAL SECURITY LAW

*July 2020*

This is a criminal book. It will stand among those now being pulled off the shelves of stores and libraries in Hong Kong. As this book goes into production, social media accounts are being scrubbed, political organizations are disbanding, and prominent activists as well as ordinary people face three impossible choices: stay and be silent; stay and be locked up; or leave for lifelong exile. Of these choices, only the first two are even feasible for the most vulnerable.

The voices preserved here would likely be found to violate the recently introduced National Security Law (NSL), which has the sweepingly absurd audacity to claim universal jurisdiction over all persons in and outside Hong Kong, whether Hongkonger or not. The NSL introduces four new crimes—secession, subversion, terrorism, and collusion with foreign forces—that are each ill-defined. It imposes up to life imprisonment, to be determined by a special scarecrow tribunal. It makes provisions for closed trials, no bail, and no jury of peers. Gazetted into law by the PRC, it was superimposed in a move bypassing Hong Kong's legislative procedure. Neither the NSL nor the secret ops department it creates within the Hong Kong Police Force are subject to Hong Kong's laws.

Barely a day after the NSL was gazetted, twenty-three-year-old medic Tong Ying-kit was arrested for driving his motorcycle through a group of police officers while bearing a popular protest flag. He was charged for secession and terrorism under the NSL. He was the first. He appeared for arraignment in a wheelchair and with broken bones. His application for bail was rejected.

Australia, Canada, and the United States have suspended their extradition treaties with Hong Kong, notwithstanding the already dubious application of the NSL to principles of international law and judicial comity. Britain and Taiwan have moved to create fast tracks to residency for those fleeing Hong Kong. It has been argued that the contemporary Hong Kong identity began to be forged in 1989, when Hong Kong transformed itself into a safe harbor for the dissidents and survivors of the Tiananmen Massacre. If that is so, then that Hong Kong identity is now a negative mirror of its own heroic beginning. It has begun its long fight against the state violence of forgetting.

Still, the protests continue. The NSL's vague, broad reach has led some to take the streets while holding up blank protest signs. The blank signs they raise are an expression of genuine uncertainty about what is now criminal or not; they are also an expression of defiance, placeholders for a multitude of words, ever immanent even if silenced.

Every page in this book bears the signature of those blank signs. If the volume of dissent and conscience must decrease in Hong Kong, that only means the volume must increase abroad. We say this knowing full well the blackmail tactics used by the PRC to threaten the families of overseas dissidents. Before the NSL, we had resolved to commit all royalty payments from this book to organizations in Hong Kong supporting the youngest of protesters cast out by both family and state. Our commitment remains the same, though those organizations are now disappearing or going underground, and though the funds will follow a narrower stream.

Watch for Hong Kong. Watch for the protest signs that go on waving: those infinitudes in the face of impossibility, those blank pages flapping like sails in the wind.

*What Persists: Selected Essays on Poetry from* The Georgia Review, *1988–2014*, by Judith Kitchen

*Conscientious Thinking: Making Sense in an Age of Idiot Savants*, by David Bosworth

*Stargazing in the Atomic Age*, by Ann Goldman

*Hong Kong without Us: A People's Poetry*, edited by the Bauhinia Project

*Hysterical Water: Poems*, by Hannah Baker Saltmarsh

*Divine Fire: Poems*, by David Woo